Printed in the United States of America

ISBN 978-0692853849

Editing: CML Collective – cmlcollective@gmail.com

THIS BOOK BELONGS TO:

This book is dedicated to all of my close family and friends. I finally did it. Thank you for all of your time and much needed support over the years. To my husband, Blake, thank you for being the reason and the very first person to breathe life into all of my dreams. For my babies, Blake II and Khaliyah, you two have always been — and will always be — the motivation for each and everything that I do. Thank you for consistently being yourselves, which is always more than enough.

To all of my brothers and sisters in arms, thank you for all that you do. I pray that this book is a blessing to all of our families.

What does your family look like?
Feel free to use this page to add a
photo of your own family!

MOMMY'S BIG TRIP

"Goodnight, moon," Liyah said as she blew kisses towards the moon.

She and her parents would take a walk each evening and say goodnight to the moon. Every evening she had a new question about the sky.

"Daddy, what are those shiny things
in the sky?" asked Liyah.
Daddy loved to hear and answer
her questions, "Those are stars, Liyah,
and they shine brightly and beauti-
fully just like you."

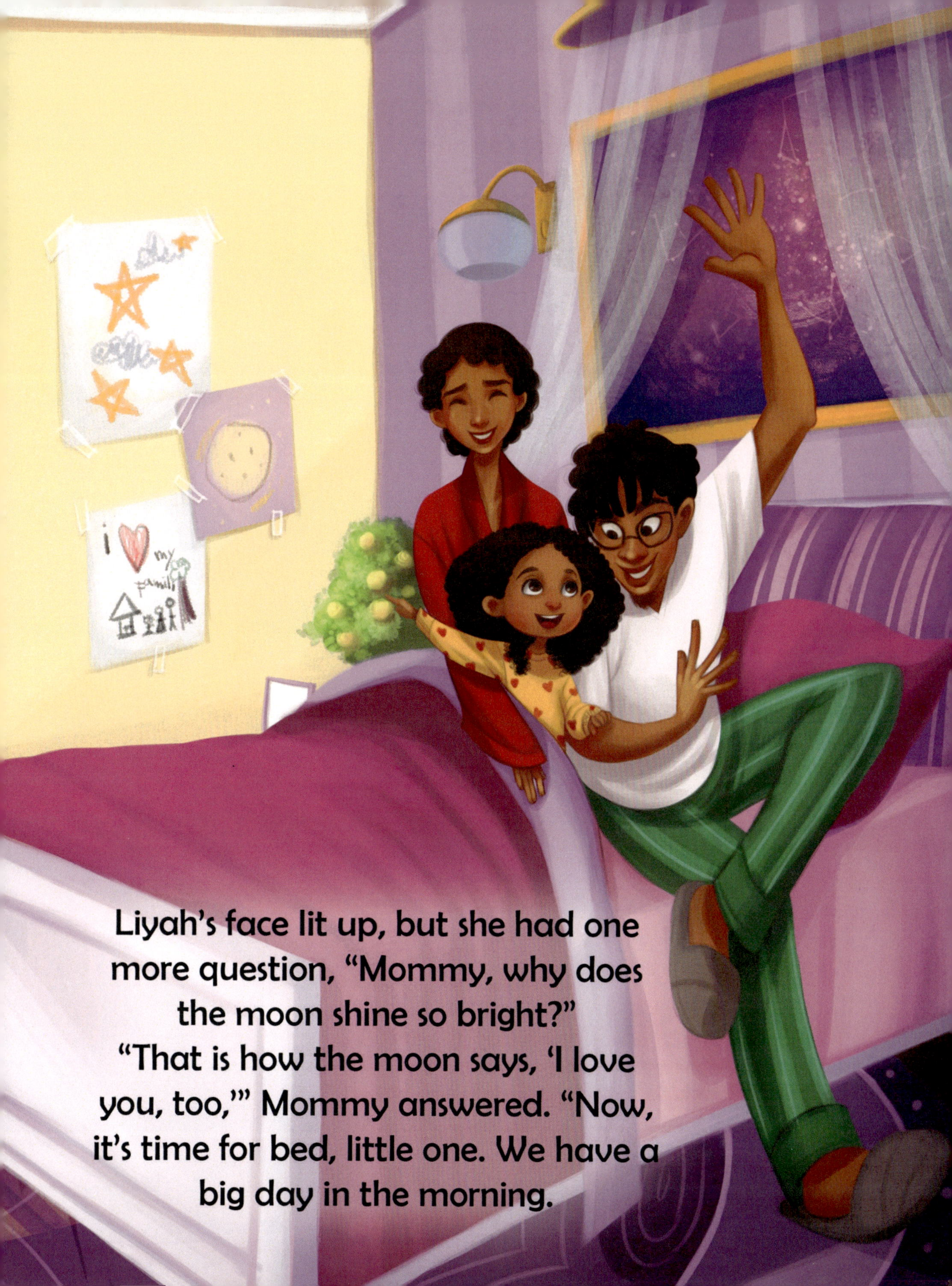

Liyah's face lit up, but she had one
more question, "Mommy, why does
the moon shine so bright?"
"That is how the moon says, 'I love
you, too,'" Mommy answered. "Now,
it's time for bed, little one. We have a
big day in the morning.

"Mommy, where are you going?" asked Liyah while watching her mother pack the following morning.

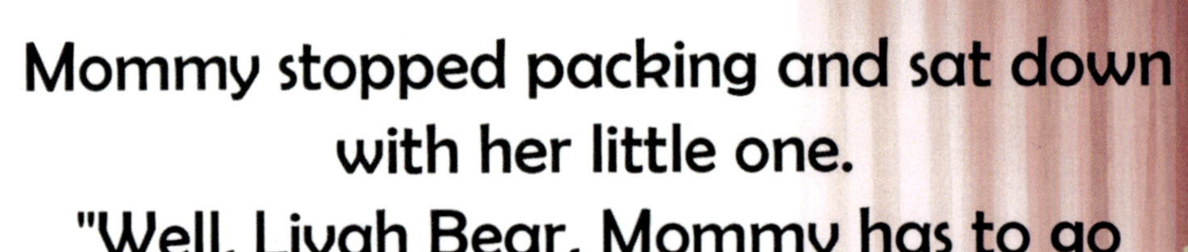

Mommy stopped packing and sat down
with her little one.
"Well, Liyah Bear, Mommy has to go
across the stars. I have to go and work,
but I'll be back to play with you again."

"Mommy, I want to go with you,"
Liyah replied with a sad voice.

All through the day, Liyah couldn't think about anything else except missing her mother. She got sad every time she saw her Mommy's packed bags sitting by the door.

That evening, Mommy took
Liyah outside into the night,
looking at the sky.
"Liyah, do you see all those
stars in the sky?"

"Yes, Mommy, I see all of them!" Liyah said excitedly. "Mommy has to go far, far across the stars. It's a very long trip. Can you count the stars in the sky?"

"One...two...three...four...five," Liyah said counting all the way to twenty. "Good job!" said Mommy, "I love you more than all those stars in the sky. When you think of me, you can come outside and count the stars."

Before long, it was time to go to bed. Mommy and Liyah both waved and blew kisses at the stars, the sky and moon and said, "Goodnight."

The next morning, Daddy helped Mommy move
her bags into the car.
Liyah was very sad. She began to remember
how she cooked with her Mommy and how
much fun they used to have during craft time.

What would her evening walks be like while her Mommy was away? Liyah knew that she would miss her Mommy very much.

Everyone got in the car to drive Mommy to the airport. It was time for her to leave for the trip.

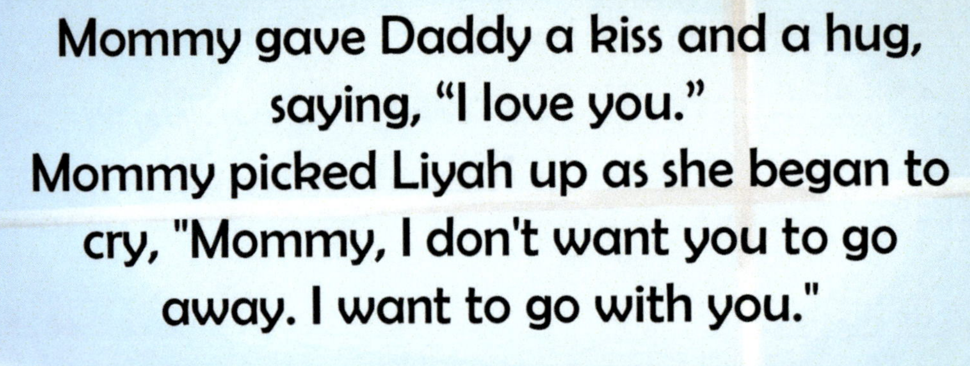

Mommy gave Daddy a kiss and a hug, saying, "I love you."
Mommy picked Liyah up as she began to cry, "Mommy, I don't want you to go away. I want to go with you."

"Oh Liyah, baby, I understand. I wish that I could take you with me, too. But, remember, I love you more than all the stars in the sky. I'll be back to see you and we'll count the stars again, together," replied Mommy.

A lot of days went by — weeks and
months, too. It seemed that Mommy
was never coming home.
Liyah really missed her Mommy.

Then, one day, Liyah came home to a huge gift box. "Open it up," Daddy said. "Mommy sent it to you." Liyah began to rip the box open, tearing off all of the tape.

'What's in the box?' Liyah thought to herself. She was always excited when Mommy sent her letters and surprises. 'What did Mommy send me this time?'

It was her Mommy!!!
Liyah was so happy and surprised that she
hugged her Mommy and would not let go.
The family was so happy that Mommy finally
returned home from her trip, but there was
one thing left to do.

They had to go on their evening walk! Liyah
could not stop smiling as she listened to
Mommy's stories from their time spent apart.
Mommy told her about how much she
missed her and how she'd look at the stars
thinking of her.

Daddy and Liyah also told Mommy how
they'd count the stars when they were sad
and wanted to see her. They all knew
that, each night, no matter how far away,
they were always together underneath
the moon and stars.

ABOUT LIYAH

Khaliyah "Liyah" Edwards is a bright and lively three-year-old girl. Like most cuddly toddlers, she loves to sing, dance, play, and make arts and crafts of all kinds. Recently, Liyah joined a group of children who have now experienced the temporary absence of a parent. She is the child of a United States Army Veteran and endured a separation from her Mother from April 2016 to January 2017. Although young Liyah recognized her mother was absent, her father, brother, grandparents, aunts and uncles took time to help her cope with the void of missing her mother. Her parents had a very hard time attempting to explain where her mother was going, why she was going and why her mother could not take her with her.

"Mommy's Big Trip" is a keepsake for all children across the world who are separated from a parent. The intent of Liyah's story is to help other children cope with an absence they may not fully understand. Liyah hopes that you enjoy her story and that she can help other children around the world who share similar experiences.

Made in the USA
San Bernardino, CA
17 March 2017